1950 U.S.

YEARBOOK

ISBN: 9781098999674

This book gives a fascinating and informative insight into life in the United States in 1950. It includes everything from the most popular music of the year to the cost of a buying a new house. Additionally, there are chapters covering people in high office, the best-selling films of the year and all the main news and events. Want to know who won the World Series or which U.S. personalities were born in 1950? All this and much more awaits you within.

INDEX

	Page
Calendar	4
People In High Office	5
U.S. News & Events	9
Worldwide News & Events	18
Births - U.S. Personalities	21
Notable Deaths	27
Popular Music	30
Top 5 Films	36
Sporting Winners	52
Cost Of Living	62
Cartoons - Comic Strips	72

FIRST EDITION

1950

January
S	M	T	W	T	F	S
1	2	3	4	5	6	7
8	9	10	11	12	13	14
15	16	17	18	19	20	21
22	23	24	25	26	27	28
29	30	31				

○:4 ☽:11 ●:18 ☾:25

February
S	M	T	W	T	F	S
			1	2	3	4
5	6	7	8	9	10	11
12	13	14	15	16	17	18
19	20	21	22	23	24	25
26	27	28				

○:2 ☽:9 ●:16 ☾:24

March
S	M	T	W	T	F	S
			1	2	3	4
5	6	7	8	9	10	11
12	13	14	15	16	17	18
19	20	21	22	23	24	25
26	27	28	29	30	31	

○:4 ☽:10 ●:18 ☾:26

April
S	M	T	W	T	F	S
						1
2	3	4	5	6	7	8
9	10	11	12	13	14	15
16	17	18	19	20	21	22
23	24	25	26	27	28	29
30						

○:2 ☽:9 ●:17 ☾:25

May
S	M	T	W	T	F	S
	1	2	3	4	5	6
7	8	9	10	11	12	13
14	15	16	17	18	19	20
21	22	23	24	25	26	27
28	29	30	31			

○:2 ☽:8 ●:16 ☾:24 ○:31

June
S	M	T	W	T	F	S
				1	2	3
4	5	6	7	8	9	10
11	12	13	14	15	16	17
18	19	20	21	22	23	24
25	26	27	28	29	30	

☽:7 ●:15 ☾:23 ○:29

July
S	M	T	W	T	F	S
						1
2	3	4	5	6	7	8
9	10	11	12	13	14	15
16	17	18	19	20	21	22
23	24	25	26	27	28	29
30	31					

☽:6 ●:15 ☾:22 ○:29

August
S	M	T	W	T	F	S
		1	2	3	4	5
6	7	8	9	10	11	12
13	14	15	16	17	18	19
20	21	22	23	24	25	26
27	28	29	30	31		

☽:5 ●:13 ☾:20 ○:27

September
S	M	T	W	T	F	S
					1	2
3	4	5	6	7	8	9
10	11	12	13	14	15	16
17	18	19	20	21	22	23
24	25	26	27	28	29	30

☽:4 ●:11 ☾:18 ○:25

October
S	M	T	W	T	F	S
1	2	3	4	5	6	7
8	9	10	11	12	13	14
15	16	17	18	19	20	21
22	23	24	25	26	27	28
29	30	31				

☽:4 ●:11 ☾:17 ○:25

November
S	M	T	W	T	F	S
			1	2	3	4
5	6	7	8	9	10	11
12	13	14	15	16	17	18
19	20	21	22	23	24	25
26	27	28	29	30		

☽:2 ●:9 ☾:16 ○:24

December
S	M	T	W	T	F	S
					1	2
3	4	5	6	7	8	9
10	11	12	13	14	15	16
17	18	19	20	21	22	23
24	25	26	27	28	29	30
31						

☽:2 ●:9 ☾:16 ○:24

PEOPLE IN HIGH OFFICE

Harry S. Truman
April 12, 1945 - January 20, 1953
Democratic Party

Born May 8, 1884, Truman served as the 33rd President of the United States succeeding to the presidency on April 12, 1945, when Roosevelt died after months of declining health. Harry S. Truman died December 26, 1972.

81st United States Congress

Vice President	Alben W. Barkley
Chief Justice	Fred M. Vinson
Speaker of the House	Sam Rayburn
Senate Majority Leader	Scott W. Lucas

U.S. Flag - 48 stars (1912-1959)

United Kingdom

Monarch
King George VI
Dec 11, 1936 - Feb 6, 1952

Prime Minister
Clement Attlee
Jul 26, 1945 - Oct 26, 1951

Australia

Canada

Ireland

Prime Minister
Sir Robert Menzies
Liberal (Coalition)
Dec 19, 1945 - Jan 26, 1966

Prime Minister
Louis St. Laurent
Liberal Party
Nov 15, 1948 - Jun 21, 1957

Taoiseach of Ireland
John A. Costello
Fine Gael
Feb 18, 1948 - Jun 13, 1951

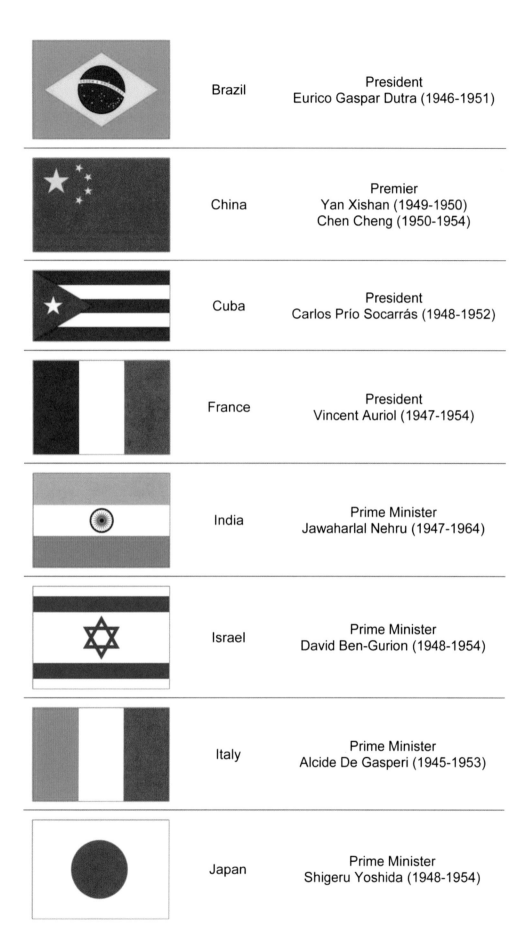

Brazil	President	Eurico Gaspar Dutra (1946-1951)
China	Premier	Yan Xishan (1949-1950) Chen Cheng (1950-1954)
Cuba	President	Carlos Prío Socarrás (1948-1952)
France	President	Vincent Auriol (1947-1954)
India	Prime Minister	Jawaharlal Nehru (1947-1964)
Israel	Prime Minister	David Ben-Gurion (1948-1954)
Italy	Prime Minister	Alcide De Gasperi (1945-1953)
Japan	Prime Minister	Shigeru Yoshida (1948-1954)

Mexico

President
Miguel Alemán Valdés (1946-1952)

New Zealand

Prime Minister
Sidney Holland (1949-1957)

Pakistan

Prime Minister
Liaquat Ali Khan (1947-1951)

Spain

President
Francisco Franco (1938-1973)

South Africa

Prime Minister
Daniel François Malan (1948-1954)

Soviet Union

Communist Party Leader
Joseph Stalin (1922-1953)

Turkey

Prime Minister
Şemsettin Günaltay (1949-1950)
Adnan Menderes (1950-1960)

West Germany

Chancellor
Konrad Adenauer (1949-1963)

U.S. NEWS & EVENTS

JAN

5	Senator Estes Kefauver introduces a resolution calling for an investigation of organized crime in the U.S.
7	A fire consumes the psychiatric building at Mercy Hospital in Davenport, Iowa, killing 40 female patients and one nurse.
17	The Great Brinks Robbery: Thieves steal more than $2.775 million from an armored car in Boston, Massachusetts - at the time it is the largest robbery in the history of the United States. Skilfully executed with few clues left at the crime scene, the robbery is billed as 'the crime of the century'. It was the work of an eleven-member gang, all of whom were later arrested.
21	T. S. Eliot's play The Cocktail Party premieres at Henry Miller's Theatre in New York City. It was the most popular of Eliot's seven plays during his lifetime and received the 1950 Tony Award for Best Play.
21	Accused communist spy Alger Hiss is convicted of perjury.

January 24: 31-year-old Jackie Robinson (the first African American to play in Major League Baseball in the modern era) signs a one-year $35,000 deal with the Brooklyn Dodgers, making him the highest paid man in history of the franchise.

25	The temperature in Cleveland reaches 73°F (23°C), a record high for the month of January.

27	The 2nd Emmy Awards (retroactively known as the 2nd Primetime Emmy Awards) are presented at the Ambassador Hotel in Los Angeles, California. Winners include Ed Wynn, the Ed Wynn Show, Milton Berle, and the comedy-variety show Texaco Star Theatre.
31	President Harry S. Truman directs the Atomic Agency Commission 'to continue with its work on all forms of atomic energy weapons, including the so-called hydrogen or super-bomb'. The orders were in response to the detonation of the Soviet Union's first atomic bomb in September 1949.

FEB

1	Green Bay Packers founder, player and coach Curly Lambeau formally resigns from the team after 31 seasons and 6 NFL titles to his credit.
2	What's My Line is broadcast for the first time on CBS-TV. The host, then called the moderator, is veteran radio and television newsman John Charles Daly.
7	The U.S. formally recognizes the State of Vietnam under leader Bảo Đại.
8	Frank McNamara and his attorney Ralph Schneider found Diners Club International with $1.5 million in initial capital. It is first independent credit card company in the world. *Fun facts: When the card was introduced Diners Club listed 27 participating restaurants and was used by just 200 of the founders' friends and acquaintances.*
9	The radioactive chemical element number 98 is synthesized for the first time by Stanley G. Thompson, Kenneth Street, Jr., Albert Ghiorso and Glenn T. Seaborg at the University of California, Berkeley.

February 9: Second Red Scare: In his speech to the Republican Women's Club at the McClure Hotel in Wheeling, West Virginia, Senator Joseph McCarthy accuses the State Department of being filled with 205 known Communists. The speech vaulted McCarthy to national prominence and sparked nationwide hysteria about subversives in the American government.

FEB

12	In an NBC News statement, Albert Einstein warns of the dangers of a nuclear arms race and calls for the peaceful coexistence of nations.
13	A U.S. Air Force Convair B-36 bomber crashes after jettisoning a Mark 4 nuclear bomb off the west coast of Canada. The USAF later stated that a fake practice core on board the aircraft was inserted into the weapon before it was dropped. This was the first such nuclear weapon loss in history.
15	Walt Disney releases Cinderella (its twelfth animated film) in Boston, Massachusetts. It becomes the greatest critical and commercial hit for the studio since Snow White and the Seven Dwarfs (1937), and helps reverse the studio's fortunes. The film later receives three Academy Award nominations, including Best Original Song for Bibbidi-Bobbidi-Boo.
23	The 7th Golden Globe Awards take place honoring the best in film for 1949. The winners include All The King's Men (directed by Robert Rossen), Broderick Crawford and Olivia de Havilland.

MAR

9	Lifelong bank robber William Francis 'Willie' Sutton, Jr. robs the Manufacturers Bank in Queens, New York. Alongside accomplices Thomas Kling and John DeVenuta, they escape with $63,933.09.
13	General Motors reports record net earnings of $656,434,232.
17	University of California, Berkeley researchers announce the creation of atomic element 98; they name it Californium.
20	Willie Sutton is added to the FBI's list of Ten Most Wanted Fugitives.

March 23: The 22nd Academy Awards ceremony is held at RKO Pantages Theatre, Hollywood, celebrating the best films from 1949. The Oscar winners include All The King's Men, Broderick Crawford and Olivia de Havilland.

APR

9   Bob Hope makes his first national television appearance on NBC as host of the variety show Star Spangled Revue.

14   NSC 68 is issued by the National Security Council. It advocates the development of the hydrogen bomb, increased military aid to America's allies, and the rollback of communist expansion.

24   Peter Pan, with music and lyrics by Leonard Bernstein, opens at the Imperial Theater on Broadway and runs for 321 performances. It stars Jean Arthur as Peter Pan, Boris Karloff in the dual roles of George Darling and Captain Hook, and Marcia Henderson as Wendy.

25   Chuck Cooper becomes the first African American drafted into the NBA when the Boston Celtics choose him as 14th overall pick.

MAY

1   Gwendolyn Brooks becomes the first African American winner of a Pulitzer Prize for her 1949 book of poetry, Annie Allen.

3   The Kefauver Committee is established to investigate organized crime in the U.S.

9   Author of science fiction and fantasy stories L. Ron Hubbard publishes Dianetics: The Modern Science of Mental Health. *Follow up: In 1952, Hubbard lost the rights to Dianetics in bankruptcy proceedings and subsequently founded Scientology. Thereafter Hubbard oversaw the growth of the Church of Scientology into a worldwide organization.*

14   German-American aerospace engineer and space architect Wernher von Braun captures the public's imagination when the Huntsville Times runs a story with the headline, "Dr. von Braun Says Rocket Flights Possible to Moon". *Fun facts: Von Braun went on to develop the rockets that launched the United States' first space satellite, Explorer 1, and was the chief architect of the Saturn V super heavy-lift launch vehicle that propelled the Apollo spacecraft to the Moon. In 1975, in recognition of his achievements, von Braun received the National Medal of Science.*

25   The Brooklyn–Battery Tunnel (officially known as the Hugh L. Carey Tunnel) is formally opened to traffic in New York City. *Fun facts: With a length of 9,117 feet (2,779m), the Brooklyn–Battery Tunnel is the longest continuous underwater vehicular tunnel in North America and is presently used by over 54,000 vehicles on an average weekday. At the time of opening the toll for using the tunnel was 35-cents.*

JUN

1   The Mauna Loa volcano in Hawaii starts erupting and soon inundates the coastal village of Hoʻokena-mauka. When the lava flows reach the ocean, they create billowy clouds of steam that rise 10,000 feet into the air. All the villagers manage to reach safety unharmed but the flows destroy about two-dozen structures and cut the highway in three places. The eruption finally ends some three weeks later on June 23.

5   The Supreme Court decides Sweatt v. Painter, successfully challenging the 'separate but equal' doctrine of racial segregation in education.

JUN

17	The first cadaveric internal kidney transplantation is performed on 44-year-old Ruth Tucker at Little Company of Mary Hospital (Evergreen Park), Illinois. Although the donated kidney is rejected 10 months later because no effective immunosuppressive drugs have yet been developed, the intervening time gives Tucker's remaining kidney time to recover and she lives another 5 years.
20	Joe DiMaggio's records his 2,000[th] hit, a seventh-inning single off Chick Pieretti, as the Yankees beat the Indians 8-2.
22	Red Channels: The Report of Communist Influence in Radio and Television is published. Issued by the right-wing journal Counterattack, the book names 151 actors, writers, musicians, broadcast journalists and others in the context of purported Communist manipulation of the entertainment industry.
27	Korean War: President Truman orders American military forces to aid in the defense of South Korea - his actions are in response to North Korean troops crossing the 38th parallel into South Korea two days earlier.
29	FIFA World Cup: The U.S. men's national soccer team defeat England 1-0 after Haitian Joseph Edouard Gaetjens scores the winning goal in Brazil. The team fail though to advance to the final round after losing to both their other Group 2 games against Spain and Chile.

JUL

5	Sixty American lives are lost at the Battle of Osan as U.S. forces enter combat for the first time in the Korean War.

July 24: A 62-feet high RTV-G-4 Bumper sounding rocket becomes the first ever rocket to be launched from Cape Canaveral.

1	Crusader Rabbit becomes the first animated series produced specifically for television. It airs on KNBH (now KNBC) in Los Angeles.
5	A B-29 Superfortress bomber carrying a Mark 4 nuclear bomb crashes shortly after take-off from Fairfield-Suisun Air Force Base in Solano County, California. Twelve men are killed in the crash, including the commander of the 9th Bombardment Wing Brigadier General Robert F. Travis, and another seven are killed on the ground 20 minutes later when the aircraft blows up after high explosives in the bomb are detonated.

August 10: The film Sunset Boulevard, directed by Billy Wilder and starring William Holden and Gloria Swanson, premieres at Radio City Music Hall in NYC. *Fun facts: The movie was nominated for 11 Academy Awards (including nominations in all four acting categories), winning three. In 1989 it was deemed 'culturally, historically, or aesthetically significant' by the U.S. Library of Congress and was included in the first group of films selected for preservation in the National Film Registry. Photo (left to right) Nancy Olson, William Holden, Gloria Swanson and Erich Von Stroheim.*

15	Ezzard Charles TKOs Freddie Beshore in 14 rounds to retain the NBA Heavyweight boxing title.
17	Korean War, Hill 303 massacre: North Korean forces fire on a group of captured U.S. soldiers killing 41. Four soldiers manage to survive by hiding under the dead bodies of the others.
22	Althea Gibson becomes the first African American tennis player to receive an invitation to compete at the U.S. National Championships. She makes her Forest Hills debut three days later on her 23rd birthday.
23	Legendary African American singer-actor Paul Robeson, whose passport has recently been revoked because of his alleged Communist affiliations, meets with officials in an effort to get it reinstated. He is unsuccessful and it is not reinstated until June 1958.

4	The comic strip Beetle Bailey is created by cartoonist Mort Walker. Today the strip is being syndicated (by King Features) in 1,800 papers around the world.

September 4: Darlington Raceway hosts the inaugural Southern 500, the first 500-mile event in NASCAR history. Packing out the stands, the 25,000 spectators were there to see the seventy-five entrants try to take their share of the $25,325 prize fund. Qualifying for the race had taken place over the course of 15 days, with future NASCAR Hall of Fame member Curtis Turner taking pole with a lap time of 82.034 seconds. The winner, by nine laps, was driver Johnny Mantz in a Plymouth. He won the race in a total time of 6h 38m 40s (averaging 75.250mph), and took home $10,510 for his first, and only, NASCAR race win.

5	Yankeetown in Florida receives 38.7 inches of rainfall as a result of Hurricane Easy, a state record.
7	The NBC radio game show Truth or Consequences debuts on CBS television. Hosted by Ralph Edwards the premise of the show was to mix the original quiz element of game shows with wacky stunts.
8	The Defense Production Act is enacted into law in response to the start of the Korean War. The Act has since been reauthorized over 50 times; it has been periodically amended, and remains in force as of 2019.
9	The state of California celebrates its centennial anniversary.
15	Korean War, Battle of Inchon: 75,000 allied troops and 261 naval vessels, commanded by Douglas MacArthur, land in North Korean occupied Inchon to begin a U.N. counteroffensive. The operation would lead to the recapture of the South Korean capital Seoul two weeks later.
21	George Marshall is sworn in as the 3rd Secretary of Defense.
23	U.S. Air Force Mustangs accidentally bomb the British 1st Battalion Argyll and Sutherland Highlanders on Hill 282 in Korea, 17 are killed.
27	NBA Heavyweight boxing champion Ezzard Charles defeats Joe Louis in 15 rounds at Yankee Stadium, Bronx, New York.

October 2: The comic strip Peanuts, written and illustrated by Charles M. Schulz, is first published in nine U.S. newspapers. *Interesting facts: At its peak in the mid to late 1960s Peanuts ran in over 2,600 newspapers and had a readership of around 355 million in 75 countries. It helped to cement the four-panel gag strip as the standard in the U.S. and, together with its merchandise, earned Schulz more than $1 billion during his lifetime. Pictured: The first ever Peanuts comic strip.*

7	The Agate Pass Bridge opens for traffic in Washington State, replacing the existing car ferry service which dated back to the 1920s. At 1,229 feet long and 75 feet above the water the bridge cost $1,351,363 to construct. In 1995 it was listed on the National Register of Historic Places.
14	The second Tacoma Narrows Bridge opens in Washington State. At 5,979 feet long it is 40 feet longer than the original bridge (which had collapsed under 40mph wind conditions on the morning of November 7, 1940).
30	The Jayuya Uprising is started by Puerto Rican nationalists who are opposed to the U.S. colonization of Puerto Rico.

NOV

1	Puerto Rican nationalists Griselio Torresola and Oscar Collazo attempt to assassinate President Truman, who is staying at Blair House in Washington, D.C. during White House repairs.

NOV

1	Celtics' forward Chuck Cooper becomes first African American to play in the NBA in Boston's 107-84 loss at Fort Wayne Pistons; future Hall of Famer Bob Cousy also debuts for the Celtics.
8	Korean War: While flying an F-80C Shooting Star, Air Force Lt. Russell J. Brown intercepts two North Korean MiG-15s near the Yalu River and shoots them down. It is the first jet-to-jet dogfight in history.
10	A U.S. Air Force B-50 Superfortress bomber experiencing engine troubles jettisons and detonates a Mark 4 nuclear bomb over Quebec, Canada (the device lacked its plutonium core).
11	Harry Hay, along with Rudi Gernreich, Dale Jennings, Bob Hull and Chuck Rowland hold the first meeting of the Mattachine Society in Los Angeles, under the name Society of Fools. It is one of the earliest LGBT (gay rights) organizations in the United States.
22	A crowd of 7,021 spectators witness the lowest ever NBA score, Ft Wayne Pistons 19, Minneapolis Lakers 18.
24	'Guys and Dolls' opens on Broadway at the 46th Street Theatre (now Richard Rodgers Theatre). It stars Robert Alda (Sky), Sam Levene (Nathan), Isabel Bigley (Sarah), and Vivian Blaine (Adelaide), and runs for 1,200 performances. It would go on to win five Tony Awards, including the award for Best Musical.
24	Great Appalachian Storm: A phenomenal winter storm ravages the north-eastern United States bringing 30 to 50 inches of snow and temperatures below 0°F. In all the storm impacts 22 states, kills 353 people and causes $66.7 million in damage ($669.59 million in 2019).
25	Korean War: Troops from the People's Republic of China, in North Korea, launch a massive counterattack against South Korean and American forces long the Ch'ongch'on River Valley. These actions dash any hope for a quick end to the conflict.
30	President Truman declines to rule out using nuclear weapons to prevent South Korea from being overrun by Chinese communist troops.

DEC

5	Ezzard Charles knocks out Nick Barone in 11 rounds in Cincinnati, Ohio to retain his World Heavyweight title.
10	Ralph Bunche becomes the first African American to be presented the Nobel Peace Prize for his late 1940s mediation in Israel.
13	19-year-old James Dean gets his first paid acting job when he makes an appearance in a Pepsi commercial.
16	22-year-old Shirley Temple announces her retirement from films after recent lacklustre performances.
16	President Truman uses the powers granted to him by the recently enacted Defense Production Act to create the Office of Defense Mobilization.
26	Gillette pay $7.37 million, in a six-year deal, for the radio and television rights to baseballs All Star and World Series games.
31	The inaugural Sebring endurance race is held at Sebring International Raceway in Florida. This first race is a six-hour race with the next race (held 14 months later) being the first 12 Hours of Sebring. The race is won by the #19 Crosley Hotshot driven by Ralph Deshon and Fritz Koster.

WORLDWIDE NEWS & EVENTS

1. January 1: The International Police Association (IPA) is founded by British police sergeant Arthur Troop (1914-2000). Today it is the largest police organization in the world with 72 national sections and over 360,000 members.

2. January 5: An Aeroflot twin-engined Lisunov Li-2 transport aircraft crashes in a snowstorm near Sverdlovsk airport in Russia. All 19 aboard are killed including almost the entire Soviet Air Force ice hockey team (VVS Moscow).

3. January 14: The Soviet MiG-17 Fresco fighter aircraft makes its maiden flight. Flown by test pilot Ivan Ivashchenko (who died two months later during testing) the aircraft eventually went into service in October 1952. Including Polish and Chinese variants, a total of 10,649 of these high-subsonic aircraft were built.

4. January 26: India promulgates its constitution and forms a republic; Rajendra Prasad is sworn in as its first president.

5. February 4: The 4th British Empire Games (now called the Commonwealth Games) opens in Auckland, New Zealand. The games were originally awarded to Montreal in Canada, and were due to be held in 1942, but had to cancelled because of World War 2.

6. February 21: The Cunard liner RMS Aquitania arrives at a scrapyard in Faslane, Scotland after having been sold to the British Iron & Steel Corporation Ltd for £125,000. The scrapping took almost a year to complete and ended an illustrious career which included steaming 3 million miles on 450 voyages. Aquitania had carried 1.2 million passengers over a period of nearly 36 years, which made her not only the longest-serving Express Liner of the 20th century but also the only major liner to serve in both World Wars. *Photo: The British ocean liner RMS Aquitania on her maiden voyage in New York (1914).*

7. | March 1: The German-born theoretical physicist Klaus Fuchs, working at Harwell Atomic Energy Research Establishment in Oxfordshire, England, is convicted (following a confession) of spying against both the U.K. and the U.S. for the Soviet Union. He is sentenced to fourteen years imprisonment but is released in 1959 after serving just nine years and four months (at the time long-term prisoners in the U.K. were entitled by law to one-third off their sentence for good behavior).

8. March 8: Carmaker Rover unveils the JET1, a revolutionary new turbine-powered concept car. It could do zero to 60mph in 14 seconds, had a maximum speed of 90mph, and could run on petrol, paraffin or diesel. A series of prototypes were made into the 1960s, but further development was dropped due too many issues in making the engines feasible for use in passenger cars. *Fun facts: After being shown in the U.K. and the U.S. in 1950, JET1 was further Improved and modified to a more aerodynamic style in 1952. It was then subjected to speed trials on the Jabbeke highway in Belgium and reached 152.691mph, a world record for a gas turbine powered car.*

9. | March 8: The first Volkswagen Type 2 (Microbus) rolls off the assembly line in Wolfsburg, Germany.
10. | March 13: In Belgium a referendum over the monarchy shows 57.7% support for the return from exile of King Léopold III.
11. | May 6: Tollund Man, a well-preserved naturally mummified corpse of a man who lived during the 4th century BC, is unearthed in Silkeborg, Denmark.
12. | May 26: Motor fuel rationing eventually comes to an end in the U.K. after it was introduced in the wake of the Second World War eleven years earlier.
13. | May 29: The Royal Canadian Mounted Police schooner St. Roch becomes the first ship to circumnavigate North America. *Interesting facts: In 1962 the St. Roch was designated a National Historic Site of Canada and can today be seen on display at the Vancouver Maritime Museum in British Columbia.*
14. | June 3: Maurice Herzog and Louis Lachenal, of the French Annapurna expedition, become the first climbers to reach a summit higher than 8,000 meters; Annapurna I in Nepal at a height of 8,091m (26,545 ft).

15.	June 25: War breaks out in Korea when troops from the North Korean People's Army, supported by the Soviet Union and China, cross the 38th parallel into South Korea.
16.	July 7: The Group Areas Act is enacted under the apartheid government of South Africa formally segregating racial groups.
17.	July 16: 199,854 soccer fans watch Uruguay defeat Brazil 2-1 to win the 1950 World Cup at the Estádio do Maracanã in Rio de Janeiro. England's George Reader, age 53, becomes not only the first Englishman to referee a World Cup Final but also the oldest match official in World Cup history.
18.	August 8: American Florence Chadwick swims the English Channel in a record time of 13 hours and 23 minutes.
19.	August 12: In his encyclical Humani generis, Pope Pius XII declares evolution to be a serious hypothesis that does not contradict essential Catholic teachings.
20.	August 15: An 8.6Mw earthquake in Assam (India) and Tibet (China) shakes the region killing approximately 4,800 people.
21.	September 3: Italian racing driver Giuseppe Farina becomes the first winner of the FIA Formula One World Championship.
22.	September 18: Rede Tupi, the first television broadcast network in South America, is founded and launched in Brazil.
23.	October 19: The People's Republic of China enters the Korean War after secretly sending thousands of soldiers across the Yalu River.
24.	November 15: An attempt to hold the Second World Peace Congress in Sheffield, England is thwarted by the British authorities who prevent many international delegates from entering the country. It is relocated to Warsaw.
25.	November 17: The 14th Dalai Lama, 15-year-old Tenzin Gyatso, assumes full temporal (political) duties after the incorporation of Tibet into the People's Republic of China.

26. December 25: The Stone of Scone, the traditional coronation stone of Scottish monarchs, English monarchs and more recently British monarchs, is stolen from London's Westminster Abbey by a group of four Scottish students with nationalist beliefs. It turns up in Scotland on the April 11, 1951. *Photo: The Stone of Scone being removed / recovered from Arbroath Abbey after being handed to the Custodian of the Abbey (James Wiseheart) by Scottish Nationalists.*

BIRTHS

U.S. PERSONALITIES

BORN IN 1950

Victoria Principal
b. January 3, 1950

Actress, entrepreneur and author born Vicki Ree Principal. She is probably best known for her role as Pamela Barnes Ewing on the primetime television soap opera Dallas; she spent nine years on the long-running series, leaving in 1987. Afterwards she began her own production company, Victoria Principal Productions, focusing mostly on television films. In the mid-1980s she became interested in natural beauty therapies, and in 1989 she created a self-named line of skincare products, Principal Secret.

Christopher Stein
b. January 5, 1950

Co-founder and guitarist of the new wave band Blondie. Stein has written / co-written many of the groups hit songs including; Sunday Girl, Heart of Glass, Dreaming, Island of Lost Souls, Rapture, and Rip Her to Shreds. Blondie has sold in excess of 40 million records worldwide and the group was inducted into the Rock and Roll Hall of Fame in 2006. In addition to his musical talents Stein is an accomplished photographer having notably taken thousands of images documenting the early New York City punk music scene.

Deborah Kaye Allen
b. January 16, 1950

Actress, dancer, choreographer, television director, television producer, and a member of the President's Committee on the Arts and Humanities. She is perhaps best known for her work on the 1982 musical-drama television series Fame, where she portrayed dance teacher Lydia Grant and served as the series' principal choreographer. In 1991 Allen was honored with a star on the Hollywood Walk of Fame and currently has a recurring role as Dr. Catherine Fox (Avery) on Grey's Anatomy.

Herbert Jackson Youngblood III
b. January 26, 1950

Former college and professional football player who was a defensive end for the Los Angeles Rams of the NFL for fourteen seasons during the 1970s and 1980s. Before playing professionally, Youngblood played college football for the University of Florida, and was recognized as an All-American. He is considered among the best players Florida ever produced. During his NFL career he was a five-time consensus All-Pro and a seven-time Pro Bowl selection. In 2001 was inducted to the Pro Football Hall of Fame.

Natalie Maria Cole
b. February 6, 1950
d. December 31, 2015

Singer, songwriter and actress who was the daughter of singer and jazz pianist Nat King Cole. She rose to success in the mid-1970s with the hits; This Will Be, I've Got Love on My Mind, and Our Love. Her success continued into the 1980s with the album Everlasting and her cover of Bruce Springsteen's Pink Cadillac. In the 1990s she released her best-selling album, Unforgettable... with Love, singing songs recorded by her father. The album sold over seven million copies and won her seven Grammy Awards.

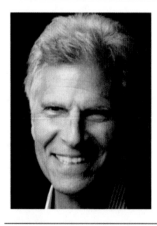

Mark Andrew Spitz
b. February 10, 1950

Former competitive swimmer and nine-time Olympic champion. After winning two team gold medals at the 1968 Summer Olympics in Mexico City, he went on to win another seven at the 1972 Summer Olympics in Munich, setting new world records in all seven events. His other achievements include an Olympic silver and bronze, five Pan American golds, 31 Amateur Athletic Union (AAU) titles, and eight National Collegiate Athletic Association (NCAA) titles. During his career he also set a total of 33 world records.

Cybill Lynne Shepherd
b. February 18, 1950

Actress, singer and former model whose better-known roles include; Jacy in The Last Picture Show (1971), Kelly in The Heartbreak Kid (1972), Betsy in Taxi Driver (1976), Maddie Hayes on Moonlighting (1985-1989), Cybill Sheridan on Cybill (1995-1998), Phyllis Kroll on The L Word (2007-2009), and Linette Montgomery on The Client List (2012-2013). Shepherd has been nominated four Emmy Awards, and six Golden Globes (of which she has won three), during her career so far.

Julius Winfield Erving II
b. February 22, 1950

Retired basketball player, commonly known by the nickname Dr. J., who helped legitimize the ABA and was the best-known player in that league when it merged with the NBA after the 1975-1976 season. Erving won three championships and four MVP Awards; he was the only player voted MVP in both the ABA and the NBA. Considered one of the most talented players in the history of the NBA, and widely acknowledged as one of the game's best dunkers, he was inducted into the Basketball Hall of Fame in 1993.

Karen Anne Carpenter
b. March 2, 1950
d. February 4, 1983

Singer and drummer, who was part of the duo the Carpenters alongside her brother Richard. The Carpenters were signed to A&M Records in 1969 and achieved commercial and critical success throughout the 1970s. After her death from heart failure, caused by complications relating to anorexia nervosa, the extensive news coverage helped increase the public's awareness of eating disorders. The Carpenters have sold more than 100 million records worldwide and are one of the best-selling music artists of all time.

James Richard 'Rick' Perry
b. March 4, 1950

Republican politician who on March 2, 2017, was confirmed by the U.S. Senate (in a 62-37 vote) as the 14th Secretary of Energy. Prior to his cabinet position Perry served as the 47th Governor of Texas from December 2000 to January 2015 - he is the longest serving governor in Texas history. Outside of politics Perry appeared on season 23 of Dancing with the Stars finishing in 12th place. He has also played himself in minor roles for several feature films and written two books.

William McChord Hurt
b. March 20, 1950

Actor whose career began on the stage in the 1970s. In 1980 he made his film debut in the science-fiction feature Altered States, for which he received a Golden Globe nomination for New Star of the Year. In 1985 Hurt garnered critical acclaim and multiple acting awards, including an Academy Award and a BAFTA Award for Best Actor, for Kiss of the Spider Woman. He has since received three additional Oscar nominations for; Children of a Lesser God (1986), Broadcast News (1987) and A History of Violence (2005).

David Bruce Cassidy
b. April 12, 1950
d. November 21, 2017

Actor, singer, songwriter, and guitarist. He was known for his role as Keith Partridge in the 1970s musical-sitcom The Partridge Family, which led to his becoming one of popular culture's teen idols and superstar pop singers of the 1970s. Ten albums by The Partridge Family and five solo albums by Cassidy were produced during the series, with most selling more than a million copies each. Cassidy became an instant drawing card with sell-out concert successes in major arenas around the world.

James Douglas Muir 'Jay' Leno
b. April 28, 1950

Comedian, actor, writer, producer and television host. After doing stand-up comedy for years he became the host of NBC's The Tonight Show with Jay Leno from 1992 to 2009, and again from 2010 to 2014. Since then Leno has maintained an active schedule as a touring stand-up comedian appearing in, on average, 200 live performances a year in venues across the United States and Canada. Leno was inducted into the Television Hall of Fame in 2014.

Stevland Hardaway Morris
b. May 13, 1950

Singer, songwriter, musician, record producer and multi-instrumentalist better known by his stage name Stevie Wonder. A child prodigy he signed with Motown's Tamla label at the age of 11. Wonder is considered to be one of the most critically and commercially successful musical performers of the late 20th century. He has recorded more than 30 U.S. top ten hits, received 25 Grammy Awards, and has been inducted into both the Songwriters and the Rock and Roll halls of fame.

Susan Kay Quatro
b. June 3, 1950

Singer, songwriter, multi-instrumentalist and actress who was the first female bass player to become a major rock star. Quatro released her eponymous debut album in 1973. Since then she has released fifteen studio albums, ten compilation albums, and one live album. Quatro has achieved her greatest successes outside the U.S. with No.1's in the U.K., Germany, Ireland and Australia with the singles; Can the Can (1973), 48 Crash (1973) and Devil Gate Drive (1974).

Hugh Anthony Cregg III
b. July 5, 1950

Grammy award winning singer, songwriter, and actor known professionally as Huey Lewis. Lewis sings lead and plays harmonica for his band, Huey Lewis and the News, in addition to writing or co-writing many of the band's songs. The band is known for their third and multi-platinum selling album Sports, and for their contribution to the soundtrack of the 1985 feature film Back to the Future. The band's two biggest selling hits, The Power of Love, and, I Want a New Drug, were both million-selling singles in the U.S.

Stephen Gary 'Woz' Wozniak
b. August 11, 1950

Inventor, electronics engineer, programmer, technology entrepreneur and philanthropist who co-founded Apple, Inc. in 1976. Both he and Apple co-founder Steve Jobs are widely recognized as pioneers of the personal computer revolution of the 1970s and 1980s. Wozniak left Apple in 1985 and founded CL 9, which in 1987 notably created the first programmable universal remote. Although he left Apple Wozniak does still today remain an employee of the company in a ceremonial capacity.

Phillip Calvin McGraw
b. September 1, 1950

Television personality, author and psychologist known as Dr. Phil. He first gained celebrity status with appearances on The Oprah Winfrey Show in the late 1990s. Oprah Winfrey then helped McGraw launch his own program, Dr. Phil, in September 2002. The Dr. Phil Show is still on the air today and is syndicated around the country. Thanks to the syndication he is one of the highest paid personalities on television. McGraw has also written several books, all of which have been commercially successful.

Joan Lunden
b. September 19, 1950

Journalist, author and a television host born Joan Elise Blunden. Lunden became the co-host of ABC's Good Morning America in 1980. She proved instantly popular and over the following 17 years reported from 26 countries, covered four presidents, five Olympic Games, and two royal weddings. After leaving GMA in 1997 she became an ABC News correspondent and has since hosted shows such as the A&E cable network program Behind Closed Doors, and A&E's Biography.

William James 'Bill' Murray
b. September 21, 1950

Actor, comedian and writer who first gained exposure on Saturday Night Live. He later starred in many popular comedy films including; Meatballs (1979), Caddyshack (1980), Stripes (1981), Tootsie (1982), Ghostbusters (1984), Scrooged (1988), Ghostbusters II (1989), What About Bob? (1991), and Groundhog Day (1993). Murray's popularity has been such that he holds an iconic status in U.S. popular culture. In 2016 he was awarded the Mark Twain Prize for American Humor by the Kennedy Center.

Patricia Lynn Murray
b. October 11, 1950

Politician serving as the senior U.S. Senator from Washington, a seat she was first elected to in 1992. A member of the Democratic Party, she is Washington State's first female Senator. She served as the Senate Majority Conference Secretary from 2007 until 2017, which made her the fourth-highest-ranking Democrat and the highest-ranking woman in the Senate. In 2017, Murray became the Senate Assistant Democratic Leader, making her the third-highest-ranking Democrat and still the highest-ranking woman in the Senate.

Thomas Earl Petty
b. October 20, 1950
d. October 2, 2017

Singer, songwriter, multi-instrumentalist, record producer and actor who was the lead singer of Tom Petty and the Heartbreakers. He was also a co-founder of the late 1980s supergroup the Traveling Wilburys. Petty recorded a number of hit singles with the Heartbreakers and as a solo artist. During his career he sold more than 80 million records worldwide, making him one of the best-selling music artists of all time. He and the Heartbreakers were inducted into the Rock and Roll Hall of Fame in 2002.

Edward Allen Harris
b. November 28, 1950

Actor, producer, director and screenwriter. His performances in Apollo 13 (1995), The Truman Show (1998), Pollock (2000) and The Hours (2002) have earned him critical acclaim in addition to Academy Award nominations. On television he is notable for his roles as Miles Roby in the miniseries Empire Falls (2005), U.S. Senator John McCain in the television movie Game Change (2012), and as the Man in Black in the HBO science fiction-western series Westworld (2016-present).

NOTABLE DEATHS

Jan 15	Henry Harley 'Hap' Arnold (b. June 25, 1886) - General Officer and aviation pioneer who is the only officer to hold a five-star rank in two different U.S. military services; General of the Army (1944-1946) and General of the Air Force (1949-1950).
Jan 22	Alan Hale Sr. (b. Rufus Edward Mackahan; February 10, 1892) - Movie actor and director most widely remembered for his many supporting character roles, in particular as a frequent sidekick of Errol Flynn.
Feb 6	Frank Gouldsmith Speck (b. November 8, 1881) - Anthropologist and professor at the University of Pennsylvania.
Feb 11	Hazen Shirley 'Kiki' Cuyler (b. August 30, 1898) - Major League Baseball right fielder from 1921 until 1938. Cuyler was inducted in the Baseball Hall of Fame in 1968.
Feb 19	Edyth Walker (b. March 27, 1867) - Opera singer who had an active international career from the 1890s through the 1910s.
Feb 25	George Richards Minot (b. December 2, 1885) - Medical researcher who shared the 1934 Nobel Prize with George Hoyt Whipple and William P. Murphy for their pioneering work on pernicious anemia.
Mar 5	Edgar Lee Masters (b. August 23, 1868) - Attorney, poet, biographer and dramatist. In all Masters published twelve plays, twenty-one books of poetry, six novels and six biographies, including those of Abraham Lincoln, Mark Twain, Vachel Lindsay and Walt Whitman.
Mar 24	James Rudolph Garfield (b. October 17, 1865) - Politician and lawyer who served as Secretary of the Interior during Theodore Roosevelt's administration. Garfield was a son of President James A. Garfield and First Lady Lucretia Garfield.
Mar 25	Frank Howard Buck (b. March 17, 1884) - Hunter, animal collector and author, as well as a film actor, director and producer. Beginning in the 1910s he made many expeditions into Asia for the purpose of hunting and collecting exotic animals. Altogether Buck is estimated to have brought back over 100,000 live specimens to the United States.
Apr 1	Charles Richard Drew (b. June 3, 1904) - Surgeon and medical researcher whose investigations in the field of blood transfusions helped develop improved techniques for blood storage. Drew applied his expert knowledge to developing large-scale blood banks early in World War II and as a consequence saved the lives of thousands of Allied forces.
Apr 3	Carter Godwin Woodson (b. December 19, 1875) - Historian, author, journalist and the founder of the Association for the Study of African American Life and History. He was one of the first scholars to study African-American history and was a founder of The Journal of Negro History in 1916. Woodson has been cited as the 'father of black history' and notably launched the celebration of Negro History Week in February 1926, the precursor of Black History Month.
Apr 11	Bainbridge Colby (b. December 22, 1869) - Lawyer, co-founder of the United States Progressive Party and the 43rd Secretary of State under President Woodrow Wilson.
Apr 22	Charles Hamilton Houston (b. September 3, 1895) - Prominent African-American lawyer, Dean of Howard University Law School, and NAACP first special counsel, or Litigation Director.

Apr 26	Hobart Cavanaugh (b. September 22, 1886) - Character actor on stage and screen who appeared in over 180 films.
May 1	Theodore Lothrop Stoddard (b. June 29, 1883) - White supremacist, historian, journalist and political scientist.
May 10	John Gould Fletcher (b. January 3, 1886) - Pulitzer Prize winning Imagist poet, author, and authority on modern painting.
Jun 22	Jane Cowl (b. December 14, 1883) - Actress and playwright notorious for playing melodramatic parts.
Jul 6	Theodore 'Fats' Navarro (b. September 24, 1923) - Jazz trumpet player who was a pioneer of the bebop style of jazz improvisation in the 1940s.
Jul 8	Helen Holmes (b. June 19, 1892) - Silent film actress most notable for starring as the quick-thinking and inventive heroine in the serial The Hazards of Helen.
Jul 10	Richard Fontaine Maury (b. December 18, 1882) - Railway engineer famous for designing the Salta-Antofagasta railway route connecting the North of Argentina with Chile across the Andes.
Jul 11	George Gard 'Buddy' DeSylva (b. January 27, 1895) - Songwriter, film producer and record executive who, alongside Johnny Mercer and Glenn Wallichs, founded Capitol Records.
Jul 12	Elsie de Wolfe, also known as Lady Mendl (b. December 20, 1860) - Actress, interior decorator, nominal author of the influential 1913 book The House in Good Taste, and a prominent figure in New York, Paris, and London society.
Jul 18	Carl Clinton Van Doren (b. September 10, 1885) - Critic and biographer who won the 1939 Pulitzer Prize for Biography or Autobiography for Benjamin Franklin.
Aug 19	Heȟáka Sápa (Black Elk) (b. December 1, 1863) - Famous medicine man of the Oglala Lakota (Sioux) who was a second cousin of the war leader Crazy Horse.
Aug 22	Kirk Bryan (b. July 22, 1888) - Geologist on the faculty of Harvard University from 1925 until his death.
Aug 23	Frank Phillips (b. November 28, 1873) - The founder of Phillips Petroleum in Bartlesville, Oklahoma (marketed as Phillips 66) in 1917, along with his brother, Lee Eldas Phillips Sr. In 2002, Phillips Petroleum merged with Conoco Oil Company and became ConocoPhillips.
Aug 25	Earl Caddock (b. February 27, 1888) - Professional wrestler and World Heavyweight Champion who was active in the early portion of the twentieth century. As the first man to bill himself as 'The Man of 1,000 Holds' (a nickname used many times since), Caddock was one of professional wrestling's biggest stars between 1915 and 1922.
Aug 26	Ransom Eli Olds (b. June 3, 1864) - Pioneer of the American automotive industry after whom the Oldsmobile and REO brands were named. He claimed to have built his first steam car as early as 1887 and his first gasoline-powered car in 1896. The modern assembly line and its basic concept is credited to Olds who used it to build the first mass-produced automobile, the Oldsmobile Curved Dash, from 1901 through 1907.
Sep 16	Pedro de Cordoba (b. September 28, 1881) - Classically trained theatre actor who appeared in numerous silent films and talkies throughout a career spanning 50 years.
Sep 23	Justin McCarthy 'Sam' Barry (b. December 17, 1892) - Collegiate coach who achieved significant accomplishments in basketball, football and baseball. Barry has been inducted into both the Naismith Memorial Basketball Hall of Fame (1979), and College Basketball Hall of Fame (2006).

Oct 7	Willis Haviland Carrier (b. November 26, 1876) - Engineer best known for inventing modern air conditioning.
Oct 13	Ernest James Haycox (b. October 1, 1899) - Author of Western fiction who published two dozen novels and about 300 short stories during his career. His story Stage to Lordsburg (1937) was made into the movie Stagecoach (1939), and featured John Wayne in the role that would make him a star.
Oct 19	Edna St. Vincent Millay (b. February 22, 1892) - Poet, playwright and feminist who received the Pulitzer Prize for Poetry in 1923.
Oct 20	Henry Lewis Stimson (b. September 21, 1867) - Statesman, lawyer and Republican Party politician. Over his long career he emerged as a leading figure in the foreign policy of the United States, serving in Republican and Democratic administrations. He served as Secretary of War (1911-1913) under William Howard Taft, Secretary of State (1929-1933) under Herbert Hoover, and Secretary of War (1940-1945) under Franklin D. Roosevelt and Harry S. Truman.

October 23, 1950 - Al Jolson (b. Asa Yoelson; May 26, 1886) - Russian-born American singer, comedian and actor who at the peak of his career was dubbed 'The World's Greatest Entertainer'. His performing style was brash and extroverted, and he popularized many songs that benefited from his shamelessly sentimental, melodramatic approach. In the 1920s Jolson was America's most famous and highest-paid entertainer but today is probably best remembered as the star of the first talking picture, The Jazz Singer.

Oct 29	Maurice George Costello (b. February 22, 1877) - Prominent vaudeville actor of the late 1890s and early 1900s, who later played a principal role in early American films as a leading man, supporting player and director.
Nov 4	Grover Cleveland Alexander (b. February 26, 1887) - Major League Baseball pitcher nicknamed 'Old Pete'. He played from 1911 through 1930 for the Philadelphia Phillies, Chicago Cubs and St. Louis Cardinals, and was elected into the Baseball Hall of Fame in 1938.
Nov 16	Robert Holbrook Smith (b. August 8, 1879) - Physician and surgeon who co-founded Alcoholics Anonymous with Bill Wilson.
Dec 4	Jesse LeRoy Brown (b. October 13, 1926) - The first African-American aviator in the U.S. Navy and a recipient of the Distinguished Flying Cross.

POPULAR MUSIC

Gordon Jenkins & The Weavers	No.1	Goodnight, Irene
Nat King Cole	No.2	Mona Lisa
Anton Karas	No.3	The Third Man Theme
Bing & Gary Crosby	No.4	Sam's Song
Bing & Gary Crosby	No.5	Play A Simple Melody
Teresa Brewer	No.6	Music, Music, Music
Guy Lombardo & His Royal Canadians	No.7	The Third Man Theme
Red Foley	No.8	Chattanoogie Shoe Shine Boy
Sammy Kaye	No.9	Harbor Lights
Sammy Kaye & Don Cornell	No.10	It Isn't Fair

N.B. The above list shows the most popular songs of 1950 according to retail sales.
Reference: Billboard magazine's 1950 year-end top 30 singles chart.

Gordon Jenkins & The Weavers
Goodnight, Irene

Label:	Written by:	Length:
Decca	Ledbetter / Lomax	3 mins 19 secs

Gordon Hill Jenkins (b. May 12, 1910 - d. May 1, 1984) was an arranger, composer and pianist who was an influential figure in popular music in the 1940s and 1950s. Jenkins discovered and was instrumental in **The Weavers (**Ronnie Gilbert, Lee Hays, Fred Hellerman, and Pete Seeger) getting a recording contract. Shortly after signing with Decca they had a 13-week run at No.1 with their release of Lead Belly's 1943 hit Goodnight, Irene.

Nat King Cole
Mona Lisa

Label:	Written by:	Length:
Capitol Records	Jay Livingston / Ray Evans	3 mins 12 secs

Nathaniel Adams Coles (b. March 17, 1919 - d. February 15, 1965), known professionally as Nat King Cole, was a singer and actor who first came to prominence as a leading jazz pianist. He was widely noted for his soft baritone voice, performing in the big band and jazz genres. In 1956 Cole became one of the first African Americans to host a national television variety show, The Nat King Cole Show (1956-1957).

3   Anton Karas
The Third Man Theme

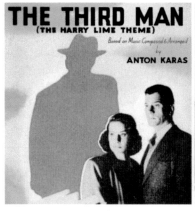  

Label:	Written by:	Length:
London Records	Anton Karas	2 mins 6 secs

Anton Karas (b. July 7, 1906 - d. January 10, 1985) was a Viennese zither player and composer, best known for his internationally famous soundtrack to Carol Reed's The Third Man (1949). The film, with the music a contributing factor, was a gigantic success, and Karas' life was changed drastically. As a result, he toured all over the world and performed for many celebrities including the British royal family.

---

4   Bing & Gary Crosby
Sam's Song

Label:	Written by:	Length:
Decca	Quadling / Elliott	2 mins 55 secs

Harry Lillis 'Bing' Crosby, Jr. (b. May 3, 1903 - d. October 14, 1977) was a singer and actor who was a leader in record sales, radio ratings, and motion picture grosses from 1931 to 1954. Crosby's trademark warm bass-baritone voice made him the best-selling recording artist of the 20th century, selling close to a billion records, tapes, compact discs, and digital downloads worldwide. Sam's Song was recorded on June 23, 1950 with his 17-year-old son **Gary Evan Crosby** (b. June 27, 1933 - d. August 24, 1995).

5 Bing & Gary Crosby
Play A Simple Melody

Label:	Written by:	Length:
Decca	Irving Berlin	2 mins 54 secs

Play A Simple Melody is a song from the 1914 musical Watch Your Step, with words and music by Irving Berlin. As with Sam's Song this duet by Bing and Gary Crosby, with Matty Matlock's All Stars, was also recorded on June 23, 1950 - it went on to peak at No.2 in the Billboard charts (these were the only two songs father and son recorded together). Gary Crosby went on to record further duets with Louis Armstrong and Sammy Davis Jr. before concentrating on his acting career.

6 Teresa Brewer
Music, Music, Music

Label:	Written by:	Length:
London Records	Weiss / Baum	2 mins 20 secs

Teresa Brewer (b. Theresa Veronica Breuer; May 7, 1931 - d. October 17, 2007) was a singer whose style incorporated country, jazz, R&B, musicals, and novelty songs. She was one of the most prolific and popular female singers of the 1950s, recording nearly 600 songs. Her No.1 hit Music, Music, Music went on to sell over a million copies and earned her the nickname Miss Music.

Guy Lombardo & His Royal Canadians
The Third Man Theme

Label:	Written by:	Length:
Decca	Anton Karas	2 mins 54 secs

Gaetano Alberto 'Guy' Lombardo (b. June 19, 1902 - d. November 5, 1977) was a bandleader and violinist of Italian descent. He formed The Royal Canadians in 1924 with his brothers Carmen (b. July 16, 1903 - d. April 17, 1971), Lebert (b. February 11, 1905 - d. June 16, 1993) and Victor (b. April 10, 1911 - d. January 22, 1994), and a number of other musicians from his hometown. Lombardo led the group to international success and they are believed to have sold between 100 and 300 million records during their lifetimes.

Red Foley
Chattanoogie Shoe Shine Boy

Label:	Written by:	Length:
Decca	Stone / Stapp	2 mins 42 secs

Clyde Julian Foley (b. June 17, 1910 - d. September 19, 1968), known professionally as Red Foley, was a singer, musician, and radio and TV personality who made a major contribution to the growth of country music after World War II. Foley has sold over 25 million records and was inducted into the Country Music Hall of Fame in 1967.

Sammy Kaye
Harbor Lights

Label:	Written by:	Length:
Columbia	Williams / Kennedy	3 mins 20 secs

Sammy Kaye (b. Samuel Zarnocay Jr.; March 13, 1910 - d. June 2, 1987) was a bandleader and songwriter whose tag line, Swing and sway with Sammy Kaye, became one of the most famous of the Big Band Era. Harbor Lights was Kaye's signature tune. It first reached the Billboard charts on September 1, 1950, lasting 25 weeks and peaking at No.1. Kaye was posthumously inducted into the Big Band and Jazz Hall of Fame in 1992.

Sammy Kaye & Don Cornell
It Isn't Fair

Label:	Written by:	Length:
RCA Victor	Himber / Warshauer / Sprigato	3 mins 18 secs

It Isn't Fair was written and published in 1933. It's revival by Don Cornell and the Sammy Kaye orchestra in 1950 has become the best-known version of the song. **Don Cornell** (b. Luigi Francisco Varlaro; April 21, 1919 - d. February 23, 2004) was a singer and vocalist in the Sammy Kaye band from the age of eighteen. He became a solo act in 1949, and between 1950 and 1962 had twelve of his records certified gold. Cornell was inducted into the Big Band Hall of Fame in 1993.

1950: TOP FILMS

1. **King Solomon's Mines** - *MGM*
2. **All About Eve** - *20th Century Fox*
3. **Cinderella** - *Disney*
4. **Annie Get Your Gun** - *MGM*
5. **Father Of The Bride** - *MGM*

OSCARS

Best Picture: All About Eve
Most Nominations: All About Eve (14)
Most Wins: All About Eve (6)

Photo 1: Presenter Gloria Swanson (left) with Best Actor / Actress winners José Ferrer and Judy Holliday. Photo 2: Joseph L. Mankiewicz - Best Director.

Best Director: Joseph L. Mankiewicz - *All About Eve*

Best Actor: José Ferrer - *Cyrano de Bergerac*
Best Actress: Judy Holliday - *Born Yesterday*
Best Supporting Actor: George Sanders - *All About Eve*
Best Supporting Actress: Josephine Hull - *Harvey*

The 23rd Academy Awards were presented on the March 29, 1951.

KING SOLOMON'S MINES

Directed by: Compton Bennett / Andrew Marton - Runtime: 1 hour 43 minutes

Adventurer Allan Quartermain leads an expedition into uncharted African territory in an attempt to locate an explorer who went missing during his search for the fabled diamond mines of King Solomon.

STARRING

Deborah Kerr, CBE
b. September 30, 1921
d. October 16, 2007

Character:
Elizabeth Curtis

Scottish film, theatre and television actress. Kerr won a Golden Globe for her performance as Anna Leonowens in The King and I, and the Sarah Siddons Award for her performance as Laura Reynolds in the play Tea and Sympathy. She was also a three-time winner of the New York Film Critics Circle Award for Best Actress and was nominated six times for the Academy Award for Best Actress but never won.

Stewart Granger
b. May 6, 1913
d. August 16, 1993

Character:
Allan Quatermain

Stewart Granger was an English film actor mainly associated with heroic and romantic leading roles. Born James Lablache Stewart, he made his film debut as an extra in The Song You Gave Me (1933). Granger was a popular leading man from the 1940s to the early 1960s, rising to fame through his appearances in the Gainsborough melodramas.

Richard Carlson
b. April 29, 1912
d. November 25, 1977

Character:
John Goode

American actor, television and film director, and screenwriter who made his acting debut on Broadway in Three Men On A Horse (1935). His first film role was in the 1938 David O. Selznick comedy The Young In Heart. From then until 1969 he went on to star in a further 55 films, mainly as a supporting actor. Carlson is perhaps best remembered for his role in the TV series I Led 3 Lives (1953-1956).

TRIVIA

Goofs | Von Brun (when Allan, Elizabeth and John first meet him) states that he hasn't seen a white face in five years, but immediately after tells them that he saw Curtis a year earlier. Neither of the three question this inconsistency.

During the stampede, when zebras run past the hiding safari members, two trucks being used to herd the animals can clearly be seen through the dust in the rear of the shot.

Interesting Facts | The Deborah Kerr character, Elizabeth Curtis, is a screenwriter's invention and does not appear in H. Rider Haggard's original novel.

CONTINUED

Interesting Facts — Errol Flynn was originally cast as Quartermain but turned it down as he did not want to sleep in a tent on location in Africa. Instead he did Kim (1950), which was filmed in India but the accommodation for the actors was at a local resort.

The scene in which Deborah Kerr cuts her own hair, and then cuts to her sunning herself with a perfectly coiffed hairstyle, got such a big laugh at the initial screenings of the film that producers debated removing the scene. However, they couldn't figure out another way to explain Kerr's change of hairstyle so they kept the improbable scenes intact.

The location footage in this film, especially the various animals, was re-used as stock footage for dozens of motion pictures in the fifties and later. This includes films such as; Tarzan, The Ape Man (1959), Watusi (1959), and the 1973 version of Trader Horn.

While filming on location in Carlsbad National Park's New Cave, Deborah Kerr took her lipstick and wrote the initials DK on a cave formation near the Klansman formation that was used as a background. An electrician also took a burned-out lamp and tossed it in a hole under that formation. Since the cave is still 'active', meaning the formations are still slowly being encased in more minerals, the initials and the lamp are now solidly encased in a layer limestone that is thin enough to see through but thick enough to prevent removal. The Carlsbad Park Rangers refer to the DK as the Deborah Kerr formation. Both are still visible to this day.

Quote — **Allan Quatermain:** ...in the end you begin to accept it all... you watch things hunting and being hunted, reproducing, killing and dying, it's all endless and pointless, except in the end one small pattern emerges from it all, the only certainty: one is born, one lives for a time then one dies, that is all...

ALL ABOUT EVE

Directed by: Joseph L. Mankiewicz - Runtime: 2 hours 18 minutes

An ingenue insinuates herself into the lives of an established but aging stage actress and her circle of theater friends.

STARRING

Ruth Elizabeth 'Bette' Davis
b. April 5, 1908
d. October 6, 1989

Character:
Margo Channing

Actress of film, television, and theater. With a career spanning 60 years, she is regarded as one of the greatest actresses in Hollywood history. She won the Academy Award for Best Actress twice, was the first person to accrue 10 Academy Award nominations for acting, and was the first woman to receive a Lifetime Achievement Award from the American Film Institute.

Anne Baxter
b. May 7, 1923
d. December 12, 1985

Character:
Eve Harrington

Actress of stage and screen. Baxter won the Academy Award for Best Supporting Actress for her role as Sophie in the 1946 film The Razor's Edge, and also received an Academy Award nomination for Best Actress for the title role in All About Eve. Other notable film performances include; The Magnificent Ambersons (1942), I Confess (1953), and The Ten Commandments (1956).

George Sanders
b. July 3, 1906
d. April 25, 1972

Character:
Addison DeWitt

British film and television actor, singer-songwriter, music composer, and author. His career as an actor spanned over forty years and included roles in films such as; Rebecca (1940), Foreign Correspondent (1940), All About Eve, for which he won the Academy Award for Best Supporting Actor, and Ivanhoe (1952). Sanders has two stars on the Hollywood Walk of Fame, for films and television.

TRIVIA

Goofs

When Karen, Bill and Margo are returning from a long weekend in the country and they run out of gas, the fuel gauge still shows that the tank is just under half full.

While Phoebe is looking at herself in the mirror during the final scene, a crew member sitting on a crane is visible for a few seconds at the top of the shot.

Interesting Facts

All About Eve shares the record for the most Oscar nominations (14) with Titanic (1997) and La La Land (2016).

CONTINUED

Interesting Facts

This was the first time two actresses from one film were both Oscar nominated for Best Actress. Anne Baxter had lobbied heavily to be nominated in the best actress category rather than as a supporting actress. By doing so she may have cost both herself and Bette Davis the award.

During the making of the film Zsa Zsa Gabor kept arriving on the set because she was jealous of her husband George Sanders in his scenes with the young blonde ingenue Marilyn Monroe.

Bette Davis fell in love with her co-star Gary Merrill during the shooting of this movie and the two married in July 1950, a few weeks after filming was completed. They adopted a baby girl whom they named Margot.

Co-star Celeste Holm spoke about her experience with Bette Davis on the first day of shooting: "I walked onto the set... on the first day and said, 'Good morning', and do you know her reply? She said, 'Oh shit, good manners'. I never spoke to her again - ever."

Years after making the picture Bette Davis said in an interview "Filming All About Eve (1950) was a very happy experience... the only bitch in the cast was Celeste Holm".

Quotes

Birdie: There's a message from the bartender. Does Miss Channing know she ordered domestic gin by mistake?
Margo: The only thing I ordered by mistake is the guests. They're domestic too, and they don't care what they drink as long as it burns!

Margo: Fasten your seatbelts, it's going to be a bumpy night!

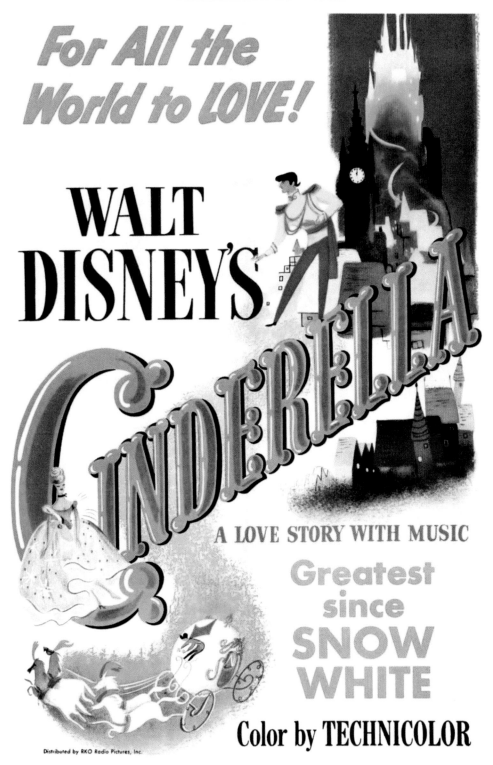

Directors: Geronimi / Jackson / Luske - Runtime: 1 hour 14 minutes

When Cinderella's cruel stepmother prevents her from attending the Royal Ball, she gets some unexpected help from the lovable mice Gus and Jaq, and from her Fairy Godmother.

STARRING

Jacqueline Ruth 'Ilene' Woods
b. May 5, 1929
d. July 1, 2010

Character:
Cinderella (voice)

Actress and singer who is primarily known as the original voice of the title character of the Walt Disney animated feature Cinderella, for which she was named a Disney Legend in 2003. The role came about when two of her songwriter friends, Mack David and Jerry Livingston, called her to record 3 songs from the film. They then presented them to Walt Disney and two days later he asked her to voice the role of Cinderella.

Eleanor Audley
b. November 19, 1905
d. November 25, 1991

Character:
Lady Tremaine (voice)

Actress who had a distinctive voice in radio and animation, in addition to her TV and film roles. She is best remembered on television as Oliver Douglas's mother, Eunice Douglas, on the CBS sitcom, Green Acres (1965-1969), and for providing Disney animated features with the villainess voices of Lady Tremaine in Cinderella (1950), and Maleficent in Sleeping Beauty (1959).

Verna Felton
b. July 20, 1890
d. December 14, 1966

Character:
Fairy Godmother (voice)

Actress who was best known for providing many voices in numerous Disney animated films, as well as voicing Fred Flintstone's mother-in-law Pearl Slaghoople in Hanna-Barbera's The Flintstones (1962-1963). Two of her other most famous roles were as Mrs. Day on The Jack Benny Program (1939-1962) and as Hilda Crocker on the CBS sitcom December Bride (1952-1959).

TRIVIA

Goofs | Whilst Cinderella is singing So This Is Love, she dips her hand the fountain wearing full-length evening gloves.

When Cinderella and the Prince are dancing, just before they go out into the garden, they cast large shadows onto the wall. These shadows do not match their movements.

Interesting Facts | The transformation of Cinderella's torn dress to that of the white ball gown was considered to be Walt Disney's favorite piece of animation.

CONTINUED

Interesting Facts

Lucifer was modeled after animator Ward Kimball's cat, a plump, six-toed calico named Feetsy. To prepare for Cinderella Kimball had studied dozens of cats but was having trouble coming up with an effective design for the villainous feline. One day Walt Disney visited the animator's home to talk shop, and Feetsy persisted in brushing against Walt's legs throughout the conversation. Walt, who was not fond of cats, finally declared, "For gosh sakes, Kimball, there's your Lucifer right here!"

Cinderella loses a shoe three times in the film: first, when she delivers the breakfast trays (causing Lucifer to look under the wrong cup), second, when she is running away from the ball, and lastly, on her wedding day running down the steps.

Ilene Woods suffered from Alzheimer's disease in the later years of her life. During this time, she did not even remember that she had played Cinderella, but nurses claimed that she was very much comforted by her song from the film, A Dream Is A Wish Your Heart Makes.

Quote

[as Cinderella prepares to try on the slipper]
Grand Duke: Come, my child.
[beckons to the Page Boy, who runs carrying the slipper. The stepmother sticks out her cane and trips him, causing the slipper to shatter into pieces]
Grand Duke: Oh, no! Oh, no, no. Oh, no. Oh, this is terrible. The King! What will he say? What will he *do*?
Cinderella: But, perhaps, if it would help...
Grand Duke: *[sobbing]* No, no, nothing can help now. Nothing!
Cinderella: [bringing out the other glass slipper] But, you see, I have the other slipper.

ANNIE GET YOUR GUN

Directed by: Charles Chaplin - Runtime: 2 hours 5 minutes

A film loosely based on the story of sharpshooter Annie Oakley and her love and professional rivalry with Frank Butler.

STARRING

Betty Hutton
b. February 26, 1921
d. March 12, 2007

Character:
Annie Oakley

Stage, film and television actress, comedian, dancer and singer born Elizabeth June Thornburg. Her film career began when she was signed by Paramount Pictures and appeared in the films The Fleet's In (1942), and The Miracle of Morgan's Creek (1944). Her biggest success though came when playing Annie Oakley in the MGM musical Annie Get Your Gun.

Harry Clifford Keel
b. April 13, 1919
d. November 7, 2004

Character:
Frank Butler

Actor and singer, known professionally as Howard Keel, who starred in a number of MGM musicals in the 1950s, and in the CBS television series Dallas (1981-1991). Success in Dallas renewed his singing career and in 1984, aged 64, he reached No.6 in the UK Albums Chart with the record 'And I Love You So'. For his contribution to motion pictures Keel received a star on the Hollywood Walk of Fame in 1960.

Louis Calhern
b. February 19, 1895
d. May 12, 1956

Character:
Buffalo Bill Cody

Stage and screen actor born Carl Henry Vogt. He began working in silent films for director Lois Weber in the early 1920s; the most notable being The Blot (1921). In 1923, Calhern left the movies to devote his career entirely to the stage, but returned after eight years with the advent of sound pictures. He was nominated for an Oscar for Best Actor for his role in the film The Magnificent Yankee (1950).

TRIVIA

Goofs | Annie sees the Statue of Liberty as she returns to America to win Frank Butler's heart. The statue wasn't completed in New York harbor until 1886, four years after Frank and Annie's actual wedding.

During the shooting match between Annie and Frank, a number of the clay targets actually explode before the shot has been taken, and several are hit despite the rifle not even pointed at the target (most noticeably on Annie's first shot). In addition, neither shooter stops to reload their rifles despite a continuous barrage of firing.

CONTINUED

Interesting Facts

Ginger Rogers wrote in her 1991 autobiography that she told her agent Leland Hayward to aggressively go after this film for her, and that money was no object. She wrote that she would have worked for one dollar to make it legal. Hayward spoke with Louis B. Mayer, who said: "Tell Ginger to stay in her high-heel shoes and her silk stockings, she could never be as rambunctious as Annie Oakley has to be".

Betty Hutton and Howard Keel did not get along during filming. Keel thought that Hutton cared more about her career than her co-stars.

Judy Garland and Frank Morgan, who appeared together in The Wizard of Oz (1939), were scheduled to reappear together in this film. Garland was fired because of health problems, and Frank Morgan died shortly after filming began. As a result of this, Betty Hutton took over Judy Garland's role as Annie Oakley, and Louis Calhern succeeded Frank Morgan as William F. Cody aka Buffalo Bill.

FATHER OF THE BRIDE

SPENCER TRACY   JOAN BENNETT   ELIZABETH TAYLOR

Father of the Bride

Directed by: Vincente Minnelli - Runtime: 1 hour 32 minutes

The father of a young woman deals with the emotional pain of her getting married, along with the financial and organisational trouble of arranging the wedding.

STARRING

Spencer Tracy
b. April 1, 1900
d. June 10, 1967

Character:
Stanley T. Banks

Spencer Bonaventure Tracy was an actor noted for his natural style and versatility. One of the major stars of Hollywood's Golden Age, he appeared in 75 films and developed a reputation among his peers as one of the screen's greatest actors. Tracy was nominated for nine Academy Awards for Best Actor, winning two and sharing the record for total nominations with Laurence Olivier.

Joan Geraldine Bennett
b. February 27, 1910
d. December 7, 1990

Characters:
Ellie Banks

Stage, film and television actress who appeared in more than 70 films over a period of 60 years. She is possibly best-remembered for her film noir femme fatale roles in director Fritz Lang's movies such as; Man Hunt (1941), The Woman In The Window (1944) and Scarlet Street (1945). In the 1960s, she achieved further success for her portrayal of Elizabeth Collins Stoddard on TV's Dark Shadows.

Elizabeth Taylor
b. February 27, 1932
d. March 23, 2011

Character:
Kay Banks

Dame Elizabeth Taylor was a British-American actress who from her early years as a child star with MGM became one of the greatest screen actresses of Hollywood's Golden Age. In total Taylor was nominated for 5 Academy Awards for Best Actress, winning on two occasions for her roles in BUtterfield 8 (1960) and Who's Afraid of Virginia Woolf? (1966).

TRIVIA

Goofs	When the Bank's are driving to meet Buckley's parents, Ellie says they are looking for the house numbered 394. When they get to the destination, the number on the house is 709.
	At the party to announce the engagement, Stanley is fixing drinks, and opens two Cokes which spray all over him. In both cases it is obvious that the spray is coming from the wall cabinet, not from the coke bottle.
Interesting Facts	Father Of The Bride was the only Best Picture Oscar nominee for 1950 not to win any Academy Awards.

CONTINUED

Interesting Facts   Spencer Tracy wanted Katharine Hepburn for his screen wife, but it was felt that they were too romantic a team to play a happily domesticated couple with children, so Joan Bennett got the part.

The premiere of this film took place six weeks after Elizabeth Taylor's real-life marriage to 'Nicky' Conrad Hilton Jr. The publicity surrounding the event is credited with helping to make the film so successful.

MGM gave 18-year-old Elizabeth Taylor a wedding gift of a one-off wedding dress designed by legendary costumier Helen Rose (a move also designed to promote the film).

Quote   **Stanley T. Banks:** You fathers will understand. You have a little girl. She looks up to you. You're her oracle. You're her hero. And then the day comes when she gets her first permanent wave and goes to her first real party, and from that day on you're in a constant state of panic.

SPORTING WINNERS

JIM KONSTANTY - BASEBALL

AP Associated Press - MALE ATHLETE OF THE YEAR

Casimir James Konstanty
Born: March 2, 1917 in Strykersville, New York
Died: June 11, 1976 in Oneonta, New York
MLB debut: June 18, 1944, for the Cincinnati Reds
Last MLB appearance: September 19, 1956, for the St. Louis Cardinals

Jim Konstanty was a relief pitcher in Major League Baseball and the National League's Most Valuable Player of 1950. He played for the Cincinnati Reds (1944), Boston Braves (1946), Philadelphia Phillies (1948-1954), New York Yankees (1954-1956) and St. Louis Cardinals (1956). Konstanty batted and threw right-handed, stood 6ft 1in tall and weighed 202 pounds.

In 1950, when the Phils 'Whiz Kids' won the National League pennant, Konstanty was named the Most Valuable Player; to date, he is the only National League relief pitcher to achieve such an honor. He appeared in 74 games (then a major league record), winning 16 games with a National League leading 22 saves. He made the NL All-Star team and received the AP Athlete of the Year and the TSN Pitcher of the Year awards.

After his baseball career Konstanty continued to operate a sporting goods store he had opened in Oneonta, New York until 1973. He also served as a minor-league pitching coach for the St. Louis Cardinals, and from 1968 to 1972 he was the director of athletics at Hartwick College in Oneonta, New York. In 2008, he was elected into the National Polish-American Sports Hall of Fame.

BABE DIDRIKSON ZAHARIAS - GOLF

AP Associated Press - FEMALE ATHLETE OF THE YEAR

Mildred Ella Didrikson Zaharias
Born: June 26, 1911 in Port Arthur, Texas
Died: September 27, 1956 in Galveston, Texas
Professional golfer from 1947 until her death in 1956

Zaharias was athlete who achieved a great deal of success in golf, basketball, baseball and track and field. At the 1932 Los Angeles Olympics she equalled the world record of 11.8 seconds in her opening heat in the 80-meter hurdles, and in the final, she broke her record with 11.7 seconds to take the gold. In the javelin she also won gold with an Olympic record throw of 43.69 meters, and took silver with a world record-tying leap of 1.657 metres (5.44 ft) in the High Jump.

It wasn't until 1935 that she began to play golf, eventually becoming America's first female golf celebrity and the leading player of the 1940s and early 1950s. In 1946 she won the U.S. Women's Amateur Golf Championship, and in 1947 she won the British Ladies Amateur Golf Championship, becoming the first American to do so. Zaharias achieved 17 straight women's amateur victories - a feat that has never been equalled. Having formally turned professional in 1947 she dominated the golfing tournaments ran by the Women's Professional Golf Association, and later the Ladies Professional Golf Association (of which she was a founding member). In 1948 she became the first woman to attempt to qualify for the U.S. Open but her application was rejected by the USGA - they stated that the event was intended to be open to men only. By 1950 she had won every golf title available. Totaling both her amateur and professional victories, Zaharias won an incredible 82 golf tournaments.

Major championships:

Women's Western Open	1940	1944	1945	1950
Titleholders Championship	1947	1950	1952	
U.S. Women's Open	1948	1950	1954	

Zaharias was the winner of the Associated Press Female Athlete of the Year a total of six times; 1932, 1945, 1946, 1947, 1950 and 1954.

GOLF

THE MASTERS - JIMMY DEMARET

The Masters Tournament is the first of the majors to be played each year and unlike the other major championships it is played at the same location - Augusta National Golf Club, Georgia. This was the 14th Masters Tournament and was held April 6-9. Jimmy Demaret won and became the first three-time Masters champion, with previous wins in 1940 and 1947. The total prize fund was $12,000, of which $2,400 went to Demaret.

PGA CHAMPIONSHIP - CHANDLER HARPER

The 1950 and 32nd PGA Championship was played June 21-27 at the Scioto Country Club in Upper Arlington, Ohio. Chandler Harper won the match play championship 4 & 3 over Henry Williams Jr. to win his only major title. The winner's share of the $17,700 prize fund was $3,500, with the runner-up receiving $1,500.

U.S. OPEN - BEN HOGAN

The 1950 U.S. Open Championship (established in 1895) was held June 8-11 at the East Course of Merion Golf Club in Ardmore, Pennsylvania. The 1948 champion Ben Hogan won the second of his four U.S. Open titles in an 18-hole playoff over 1946 champion Lloyd Mangrum and George Fazio, just 16 months after being severely injured in an automobile accident. It was the fourth of Hogan's nine major titles. The total prize fund was $15,000, of which Hogan took home $4,000.

Ben Hogan

Chandler Harper

Jimmy Demaret

WORLD SERIES - NEW YORK YANKEES

New York Yankees   4 - 0   **Philadelphia Phillies**

Total attendance: 196,009 - Average attendance: 49,002
Winning player's share: $5,738 - Losing player's share: $4,081

The World Series is the annual championship series of Major League Baseball. Played since 1903 between the American League champion team and the National League champion, it is determined through a best-of-seven playoff.

The 1950 World Series matched the New York Yankees against the Philadelphia Phillies. The Yankees won their 13th championship in their 41-year history, taking the Series in a four-game sweep. The 1950 World Series title would be the second of a record five straight titles for the New York Yankees (1949-1953). This was also the last all-white World Series as neither club had integrated in 1950. It was also the last World Series where television coverage was pooled between the four major networks of the day: that season, the Mutual Broadcasting System, who had long been the radio home for the World Series, purchased the TV rights despite not (and indeed, never) having a television network. They would eventually sell on the rights to NBC, beginning a long relationship with the sport.

	Date	Score			Location	Time	Att.
1	Oct 4	**Yankees**	1-0	Phillies	Shibe Park	2:17	30,746
2	Oct 5	**Yankees**	2-1	Phillies	Shibe Park	3:06	32,660
3	Oct 6	Phillies	2-3	**Yankees**	Yankee Stadium	2:35	64.505
4	Oct 7	Phillies	2-5	**Yankees**	Yankee Stadium	2:05	68.098

HORSE RACING

Hill Prince and jockey Eddie Arcaro in the winner's circle at Preakness in 1950.

Hill Prince (1947-1970) was an American Thoroughbred racehorse. He was one of the leading American two-year-olds of 1949, alongside Oil Capitol and Middleground. In 1950, he ran fifteen times, winning races including the Preakness Stakes, Wood Memorial Stakes, Withers Stakes, American Derby, Jockey Club Gold Cup, Jerome Handicap and Sunset Handicap, and was named American Horse of the Year. In 1991 Hill Prince was inducted into the National Museum of Racing and Hall of Fame.

KENTUCKY DERBY - MIDDLEGROUND

The Kentucky Derby is held annually at Churchill Downs in Louisville, Kentucky on the first Saturday in May. The race is a Grade 1 stakes race for three-year-olds and is one and a quarter mile in length.

PREAKNESS STAKES - HILL PRINCE

The Preakness Stakes is held on the third Saturday in May each year at Pimlico Race Course in Baltimore, Maryland. It is a Grade 1 race run over a distance of 9.5 furlongs (1 3/16 mile) on dirt.

BELMONT STAKES - MIDDLEGROUND

The Belmont Stakes is Grade 1 race held every June at Belmont Park in Elmont, New York. It is 1.5 mile in length and open to three-year-old thoroughbreds. It takes place on a Saturday between June 5 and June 11.

FOOTBALL - NFL CHAMPIONSHIP

CHAMPIONSHIP GAME

Los Angeles Rams   28 - 30   **Cleveland Browns**

Played: December 24, 1950 at Cleveland Stadium, Cleveland, Ohio
Attendance: 29,751 - Winning player's share: $1,113 - Losing player's share: $686

The 1950 National Football League Championship Game was the 18th title game for the NFL and featured the American Conference champion Cleveland Browns against the National Conference winners Los Angeles Rams.

Season Standings:

American Conference

Pos.	Team	P	W	L	T	PCT	PF	PA
1st	**Cleveland Browns**	**12**	**10**	**2**	**0**	**.833**	**310**	**144**
2nd	New York Giants	12	10	2	0	.833	268	150
3rd	Philadelphia Eagles	12	6	6	0	.500	254	141
4th	Pittsburgh Steelers	12	6	6	0	.500	180	195
5th	Chicago Cardinals	12	5	7	0	.417	233	287

National Conference

Pos.	Team	P	W	L	T	PCT	PF	PA
1st	**Los Angeles Rams**	**12**	**9**	**3**	**0**	**.750**	**466**	**309**
2nd	Chicago Bears	12	9	3	0	.750	279	207
3rd	New York Yanks	12	7	5	0	.583	366	367
4th	Detroit Lions	12	6	6	0	.500	321	285
5th	Green Bay Packers	12	3	9	0	.250	244	406

League Leaders

Statistic	Name	Team	Yards
Passing	Bobby Layne	Detroit Lions	2323
Rushing	Marion Motley	Cleveland Browns	810
Receiving	Tom Fears	Los Angeles Rams	116

The 1950 NFL season was the 31st regular season of the National Football League. The merger with the All-America Football Conference (AAFC) expanded the league to 13 teams and television brought a new era to the game.

HOCKEY: 1949-50 NHL SEASON

The 1949-50 NHL season was the 33rd season of the National Hockey League and included six teams each playing 70 games. In the Stanley Cup the Detroit Red Wings defeated the New York Rangers in seven games to win their fourth championship.

Final Standings:

Pos.	Team	GP	W	L	T	GF	GA	Pts
1st	**Detroit Red Wings**	**70**	**37**	**19**	**14**	**229**	**164**	**88**
2nd	Montreal Canadiens	70	29	22	19	172	150	77
3rd	Toronto Maple Leafs	70	31	27	12	176	173	74
4th	New York Rangers	70	28	31	11	170	189	67
5th	Boston Bruins	70	22	32	16	198	228	60
6th	Chicago Black Hawks	70	22	38	10	203	244	54

Scoring Leaders

	Player	Team	Goals	Assists	Points
1	**Ted Lindsay**	**Detroit Red Wings**	**23**	**55**	**78**
2	Sid Abel	Detroit Red Wings	34	35	69
3	Gordie Howe	Detroit Red Wings	35	33	68

Hart Trophy (Most Valuable Player): Charlie Rayner, New York Rangers
Vezina Trophy (Fewest Goals Allowed): Bill Durnan - Montreal Canadiens

STANLEY CUP

Detroit Red Wings	4 - 3	New York Rangers

Series Summary

	Date	Team	Result	Team	Stadium
1	Apr 11	New York Rangers	1-4	Detroit Red Wings	Olympia Stadium
2	Apr 13	Detroit Red Wings	1-3	New York Rangers	Maple Leaf Gardens
3	Apr 15	Detroit Red Wings	4-0	New York Rangers	Maple Leaf Gardens
4	Apr 18	New York Rangers	4-3 (OT)	Detroit Red Wings	Olympia Stadium
5	Apr 20	New York Rangers	2-1 (OT)	Detroit Red Wings	Olympia Stadium
6	Apr 22	New York Rangers	4-5	Detroit Red Wings	Olympia Stadium
7	Apr 23	New York Rangers	3-4 (2OT)	Detroit Red Wings	Olympia Stadium

INDIANAPOLIS 500 - JOHNNIE PARSONS

The 34th International 500-Mile Sweepstakes Race was held at the Indianapolis Motor Speedway on Tuesday, May 30, 1950. The race was won by Johnnie Parsons in front of a crowd of 175,000 spectators; Bill Holland came second and Mauri Rose third. The race was originally scheduled for 200 laps (500 miles), but was stopped after 138 laps (345 miles) due to rain. *Fun fact: Johnnie Parsons has the dubious distinction of being the only Indianapolis 500 winner to have his name misspelled on the Borg-Warner Trophy. The silversmith carved 'Johnny' instead of 'Johnnie'.*

BOSTON MARATHON KEE YONG HAM

The Boston Marathon is the oldest annual marathon in the world and dates back to 1897.

Race Result:

1st	**Kee Yong Ham**	**South Korea**	**2:32:39**
2nd	Ki Yoon Song	South Korea	2:35:58
3rd	Yun Chi Choi	South Korea	2:39:47

BASKETBALL - NBA FINALS

4 - 2

Minneapolis Lakers   Syracuse Nationals

LEAGUE SUMMARY

The 1949-50 NBA season was the inaugural season of the National Basketball Association, which was created in 1949 by merger of the 3-year-old BAA and 12-year-old NBL.

Eastern Division

Pos.	Team	GP	W	L	PCT	GB
1st	**Syracuse Nationals**	**64**	**51**	**13**	**.797**	-
2nd	New York Knicks	68	40	28	.588	13
3rd	Washington Capitols	68	32	36	.471	21

Central Division

Pos.	Team	GP	W	L	PCT	GB
1st	**Minneapolis Lakers**	**68**	**51**	**17**	**.750**	-
2nd	Rochester Royals	68	51	17	.750	-
3rd	Fort Wayne Pistons	68	40	28	.588	11

Western Division

Pos.	Team	GP	W	L	PCT	GB
1st	**Indianapolis Olympians**	**64**	**39**	**25**	**.609**	-
2nd	Anderson Packers	64	37	27	.578	2
3rd	Tri-Cities Blackhawks	64	29	35	.453	10

Statistics Leaders

	Player	Team	Stats
Points	George Mikan	Minneapolis Lakers	1,865
Assists	Dick McGuire	New York Knicks	386
FG%	Alex Groza	Indianapolis Olympians	.478
FT%	Max Zaslofsky	Chicago Stags	.843

Note: Prior to the 1969-70 season league leaders in points and assists were determined by totals rather than averages.

TENNIS - U.S. NATIONAL CHAMPIONSHIPS

Mens Singles Champion - Art Larsen - United States
Ladies Singles Champion - Margaret Osborne duPont - United States

The 1950 U.S. National Championships (now known as the U.S. Open) took place on the outdoor grass courts at the West Side Tennis Club, Forest Hills in New York. The tournament ran from August 25 until September 5, and was the 70th staging of the U.S. National Championships.

Men's Singles Final

Country	Player	Set 1	Set 2	Set 3	Set 4	Set 5
United States	Art Larsen	6	4	5	6	6
United States	Herb Flam	3	6	7	4	3

Women's Singles Final

Country	Player	Set 1	Set 2
United States	Margaret Osborne duPont	6	6
United States	Doris Hart	3	3

Men's Doubles Final

Country	Players	Set 1	Set 2	Set 3	Set 4
Australia	John Bromwich / Frank Sedgman	7	8	3	6
United States	Bill Talbert / Gardnar Mulloy	5	6	6	1

Women's Doubles Final

Country	Players	Set 1	Set 2
United States	Louise Brough / Margaret Osborne duPont	6	6
United States	Shirley Fry / Doris Hart	2	3

Mixed Doubles Final

Country	Players	Set 1	Set 2	Set 3
United States / Australia	Margaret Osborne duPont / Ken McGregor	6	3	6
United States / Australia	Doris Hart / Frank Sedgman	4	6	3

THE COST OF LIVING

COMPARISON CHART

	1950	1950 + Inflation	2019	% Change
House	$15,200	$160,327	$309,700	+93.2%
Annual Income	$1,800	$18,986	$61,372	+223.2%
Car	$2,250	$23,733	$34,000	+43.3%
Gallon of Gasoline	26¢	$2.74	$2.70	-1.5%
Gallon of Milk	30¢	$3.16	$3.28	+3.8%
DC Comic Book	10¢	$1.05	$3.99	+280%

GROCERIES

Mrs Wrights Bread (24oz loaf)	18¢
Sunshine Crackers (1lb box)	25¢
Parkay Margarine (per lb)	39¢
Red & White Milk (tall can)	10¢
Large Fresh Country Eggs (dozen)	29¢
Wisconsin Cheese (per lb)	43¢
Imperial Cane Sugar (5lb)	43¢
Sunnyfield White Flour (10lbs)	75¢
Ann Page Peanut Butter (1lb jar)	39¢
Dried Apples (per lb)	25¢
Oranges (5lb bag)	45¢
Sunkist Lemons (per lb)	12¢
Grapefruit (2lbs)	19¢
Donna Dean Strawberries (per lb)	49¢
Fresh Tomatoes (crate)	19¢
Russets Potatoes (10lbs)	55¢
New Potatoes (2lbs)	15¢
Corn (6 ears)	25¢
Green Cabbage (per lb)	4¢
Burmuda Onions (3lbs)	10¢
Carrots (2x large bunch)	13¢
Sirloin Steak (per lb)	89¢
Baby Beef Square Cut Shoulder Roast (per lb)	59¢
Leg Of Lamb (per lb)	69¢
Cudahy Tenderized Ham (per lb)	39¢
Pig Liver (per lb)	25¢
Armour's Star Bacon (per lb)	59¢
Full Dressed Fryers (per lb)	65¢
Armour's Corned Beef Hash (16oz can)	33¢
Ranch Style Beans (2 cans)	25¢
Del Monte Ketchup (14oz bottle)	19¢
Ann Page Chili Sauce (12oz bottle)	25¢
Edwards Coffee (1lb can)	73¢
Nob Hill Coffee (1lb pkg)	68¢
Maxwell House Tea (¼lb pkg)	27¢
Coca-Cola (6 bottles)	25¢
Dr Pepper (6 bottles)	25¢
Florida Gold Orange Juice (46oz can)	25¢
Campbell's Tomato Juice (46oz can)	29¢
Snow Clouds Marshmallows (8oz pkg)	10¢
Liggett's Chocolate Bar (3x jumbo size)	43¢
Halo Shampoo	79¢
Dorothy Perkins Cream Deodorant	50¢
Waldorf Tissue (3 rolls)	20¢
Colgate Toothpaste	27¢
Listerine	69¢
Bayer Aspirin (100)	43¢
Ruffy Dog Food (15oz can)	5¢

only

PERMA·LIFT

gives you

"The Lift That Never Lets You Down"

Look for the  *Magic Inset*

Because you love to look lovely, you must wear a "Perma•lift"* Bra. Delicately designed to assure the fashion favored curves you crave, it magically, lastingly supports your breasts from below. Wash it, wear it—the Magic Insets lift you always. Select the style just made for you—at your favorite corset department. Priced so low you can afford several—$1.25 to $5.

For comfort beyond compare, wear a "Perma•lift" Magic Inset Girdle—No Bones About It—Stays Up Without Stays.

Perma·lift
REG. U. S. PAT. OFF.
BRASSIERES
THE LIFT THAT NEVER LETS YOU DOWN

"Perma·lift" is a trademark of A. Stein & Company—(Reg. U. S. Pat. Off.)

CLOTHES

Women's Clothing

Penney's Wool Winter Coat	$14
Pure Silk Scarf	$1.98
Sears Spring Suit	$12
Marks Bros. Warm Weather Dress	$17.95
Penney's Cotton Pique Dress	$3.98
J. M. Dyer Broadcloth Shirt	$3.95
Batiste Blouse	$2.98
Salle-Ann Rayon Crepe Robe	$8.98
Marks Bros. Slip	$1.95
Vanity Fair Nylon Panties	$1.75
Nylon Sheers	$1.65
Hill & Shipe Deb Shoes	$7.95
Vamp Sandals	$2.98
J. M. Dyer Lounge Slippers	$1

Men's Clothing

Sears Leather Surcoat	$19.99
P. Samuels Sports Jacket	$25
Penney's Panama Hat	$3.98
Worsted Sharkskin Suit	$45
Van Heusen Sport Shirt	$4.95
Pilgrim Tie	77¢
P. Samuels Slacks	$6.90
K. Wolens Flannel Pajamas	$2.98
Macrays Leather Oxford Shoes	$5.88
Army Shoes	$4.95
Rayon Sox (4 pairs)	$1

66

TOYS

Murray-Ohio16in Bicycle	$29.95
Pedal Police Car	$15.45
Musical Hobby Horse	$1.49
Steel Coaster Wagon	$4.95
American Flyer Freight Train Set	$15.95
Champion Roller Skates	$1.79
Doll Carriage	$5.95
Toni 16in Doll	$11.98
Horseman Tiny Baby Doll	$5.98
Susie Goose Cleaning Set	$1.75
Toy Phone	$1.19
Junior Miss Cosmetic Set	95¢
Gilbert Chemistry Set	$7.95
Football	$2.59
Football Helmet	$2.79
Basketball	$4.98
Tom Thumb Cash Register	$2.95
Cowboy Suit	$4.95
Cowgirl Suit	$3.95
Texas Junior Six Shooter	98¢
Gene Autrey Boots	$3.98
ABC Blocks	65¢

OTHER ITEMS

Cadillac Series 62 Ragtop	$3,654
Buick Super	$2,139
Dodge Wayfarer 3 Passenger Coupe	$1,611
Goodyear Deluxe Tires (6.00x16)	$15.80
Magic Chef Gas Range	$149.50
Westinghouse 12½in Television	$299.95
Firestone 8cu.ft. Refrigerator	$194.95
Coldspots 7.5cu.ft. Chest Freezer	$166.66
Kenmore Tank-Type Vacuum Cleaner	$38.88
Truetone Portable Radio	$27.95
Automatic Electric Coffee Maker	$9.50
Sears Pop-Up Toaster	$17.95
J. C. Higgins Shotgun	$75
H&R Heavy .22 Single Shot Rifle	$14.95
Ballantine's Scotch Whiskey (4/5 quart)	$5.75
Old Stagg Kentucky Straight Bourbon (4/5 quart)	$3.95
Leading Brands Cigarettes (pack)	34¢

Best Ride Money can Buy*

Costs a Lot Less Money**

when you go GREYHOUND!

MONEY CONVERSION TABLE

Amount	1950	2019
Penny	1¢	11¢
Nickel	5¢	53¢
Dime	10¢	$1.06
Quarter Dollar	25¢	$2.65
Half Dollar	50¢	$5.30
Dollar	$1	$10.60
Two Dollars	$2	$21.21
Five Dollars	$5	$53.02
Ten Dollars	$10	$106.04
Twenty Dollars	$20	$212.07
Fifty Dollars	$50	$530.18
One Hundred Dollars	$100	$1,060.37

U.S. COINS

Official Circulated U.S. Coins		Years Produced
Half-Cent	½¢	1792 - 1857
Cent (Penny)	1¢	1793 - Present
2-Cent	2¢	1864 - 1873
3-Cent	3¢	1851 - 1889
Half-Dime	5¢	1792 - 1873
Five Cent Nickel	5¢	1866 - Present
Dime	10¢	1792 - Present
20-Cent	20¢	1875 - 1878
Quarter	25¢	1796 - Present
Half Dollar	50¢	1794 - Present
Dollar Coin	$1	1794 - Present
Quarter Eagle	$2.50	1792 - 1929
Three-Dollar Piece	$3	1854 - 1889
Four-Dollar Piece	$4	1879 - 1880
Half Eagle	$5	1795 – 1929
Commemorative Half Eagle	$5	1980 - Present
Silver Eagle	$1	1986 - Present
Gold Eagle	$5	1986 - Present
Platinum Eagle	$10 - $100	1997 - Present
Double Eagle (Gold)	$20	1849 - 1933
Half Union	$50	1915

Studebaker Commander convertible

White sidewall tires and wheel discs optional at extra cost.

This "next look" in cars is a "jet-propelled" look!

ALL AMERICA is intensely excited about this aerodynamic new 1950 Studebaker.

Most people say it's so startling a car, they half expect to see it take off and fly!

It's a 1950 Studebaker just as far-advanced in engineering as it is in "next look" styling.

No bulging bulk burdens that trim, sleek, flight-streamed Studebaker structure.

This results in savings of poundage that save you plenty of gasoline mile after mile.

Stop in at a showroom. Take a close-up look at this 1950 Studebaker "next look" in cars.

See America's most distinctive sedans, coupes, convertibles.

New 1950 Studebaker
Styled ahead for years to come!

CARTOONS - COMIC STRIPS

"Take your foot off it!"

"Cracked engine-block? That's a relief. I thought
sure it was a leaky radiator."

72

Made in the USA
Monee, IL
02 June 2020